D1084596

Riversongs

Other books by Michael Anania

The Color of Dust (1970)
Set/Sorts, chapbook (1974)
New Poetry Anthology, editor (1969)

MICHAEL ANANIA

Riversongs

University of Illinois Press / *Urbana Chicago London*

12/1978
Am. Lit.

Grateful acknowledgment is made to the following publications in which some of these poems first appeared: *Stash, Prism/International, Oyez Review, Vortex, P.E.N. Quarterly, Lorax, New Collages, Portland State Review, Chicagoland, Inscape, Poetry, Mojo Navigator(e), Poetry Now, Syncline, Annex 21,* and *Tri-Quarterly.* "Riversong IX," "Reeving," and "Return" were published in *Heartland II* (Northern Illinois University Press). "Lumen" was first published as a broadside by The Wine Press, and "News Notes, 1970" first appeared as a poster poem published by Savage and Savage. *Set/Sorts* first appeared as a Wine Press Chapbook.

"A Hanging Screen," "Materials of June," and "Afternoons" were published in *Poetry* (copyright 1975 by The Modern Poetry Association), as was "Esthétique du Râle" (copyright 1977 by The Modern Poetry Association).

Some of the poems in this collection were written, in whole or in part, while I was in residence at the Roadstead Foundation in Fish Creek, Wisconsin.

Library of Congress Cataloging in Publication Data

Anania, Michael, 1939–
  Riversongs.

  I. Title.
PS3551.N25R5   811'.5'4   78-12900
ISBN 0-252-00717-4
ISBN 0-252-00718-2 pbk.

for Francesca,
who dances here

Contents

I

The Riversongs of Arion, I-X

"The Rule is one, like itself accompanied with stability and rest; if once we go astray from that, there is neither end nor quiet in error, but restlessness and emptiness."

Thomas Hooker (1659)

"This evening Guthrege Cought a *White Catfish* . . . tale much like that of a *Dolfin.*"

Journals of Lewis and Clark
(July 24, 1804)

For notes on the backgrounds of this sequence see "On 'The Riversongs of Arion,'" pp. 85-86.

I

Adrift on an oil-drum raft
I have traveled this river south
past packinghouse spills

with split-bellied watermelons
and castaway chicken heads.
I have seen catfish and bullheads

feed among the scum that eddies
beneath eroded silt shoals
and heard the silver tankers

taxi across crestfallen bluffs
at the fenced bend above the Platte's
mouth and caught, now, at midstream

on a rusted snare of dredge cable
with the slow brown water curling
dark foam against barrel heads,

my fingers track the grain of dry plank,
measuring the dull cadence of bare
feet over a worn poler's tread.

II

The river's wavelets,
thick with sewage, move,
it seems, upstream against

final deposit in some
widening delta. Illusive.
It is the rush beneath

speeding as the deep
channel bends; the surface
moving more slowly, inertial,

is curled back and downward.
So, when catfish feed
in quick channel waters,

they move upstream, angling
into the surface just as
the curling wave is pulled

back. Rivermen call this
the catfish dance because
from the banks they seem

stationary, bobbing up
and down in the dark foam.
Marquette feared the thud

of their bodies against
his canoe; treacherous,
the roiling brown waters,

Pekitanoui, route to
the vermillion sea, with
large branches, whole trees

adrift, floating islands,
the channel blue, called
ponderosa. Goodrich's white?

a common channel cat, up to
four feet, *punctatus*. I wait.
White Catfish Camp—that stretch

of silt, as good as any, any
song, river, now, like furrowed
loam, dendrite bluffs. They leap.

III   ("the always restless, always moving on")

Some years before set
forth by raft across
the oil-slick sludge
of Angel Lake, SE
off Locust Street
toward Paxton-Vierling
and the U.P. Shops.

He called himself The Kid,
said: Like The Kid don't
take no shit from nobody.
Said: Like don't nobody
fuck with The Kid.

The print of black water
along his arm, each pore
webbed with it, and washed
up over the packing-crate lid,
coming closer each time
he moved—THIS SIDE UP.
Locust Street viaduct behind
him, the freightyard, rail-
head pennies spread like leaves;
to the left, the drive-in movie
angling east; beam crane dead
ahead; windward, the city,
odors of cattle across steel.

The cool he put on
each morning, uneasy,
adjusted all day,
his arduous slouch,
flared cuffs, hair
oiled and arched back.

Somewhat confused, the surface
so much like creosote on wood,
and the evening closing down.
It was not what he had imagined,
night along the cinder shore,
hardly angelic, not a lake at all,
and the movie slivering its wedge
of light against tarnished silver,
his line of sight down the edge
of it—indistinguishable bright
objects, Monument Valley, perhaps,
thin strands of horses spilling
toward him like kelp in the crests
of long, persistent waves—the West,
Terminus, repeated everywhere, light
of the Rockies jostled with these
shadows, "never to be thrown down."

It was in Lincoln County,
the Lincoln County Wars, he
carved his name; in Texas
against carpetbaggers, home-
stead plundered, fiancé
promised to a storekeeper;
in Abilene against Hickok;
greased lightning; Vera Cruz,
that sunny afternoon, a smile;
"two sixes to beat," aces and eights
with his back to the door.

The sun hovers, cloudless sky,
town caught in its shadows,
a mother sweeps her child
away, curtains twitch, unseen
eyes, horseflesh ripples;

9

thin fingers that dealt smart
faro, cigar cupped in his hand;
it went to his lips, a shade slow,
the other, and fell for a border roll.

"I got no quarrel with you, Kid,"

so pulled her up into the saddle
behind him and rode away. How
sudden that sunset, saguaros.

Nowhere to go, riversump among refuse,
and under a ridge of pebbled glass—
skylights sooted dark as shale—
the Shops' nightsong, Union Pacific
hammered out "its dead indifference."

Dumbass, he said, skidding home,
loose heel-cleat scything his ankle.

IV

Dark-skinned with black hair
drawn tightly back, looking
northward through clay-ribbed
bluffs, she stood, I think,
ahead of the polers
in the keelboat's blunt
wet prow with a Yankee
helmsman facing her back,

and the wind, westerly—
out of my own childhood
and that unbroken prairie
where the Pawnee moved
like dust—shook the chewed
fringes of her buckskin dress.

    ". . . these barbary coasts . . ."

Stiff chokecherry thickets,
quick with sparrows, high
grasses where gray slag cuts
back to rain slides of yellow clay.
The same shores—or not? In time
the river sidewinds its banks.
Never the same soil; here, marks
of the land's uneven flow.

All fancy. She did not pass here,
met them half-a-year north,
already with child—Baptiste,
called Pomp, for Pompey—
with Lewis attending his birth,

". . . having the rattle of a snake by me
I gave it to him and he administered two
rings of it to the woman broken in small
pieces with the fingers and added to a
small quantity of water. . . ."

yet the fringes, like pinfeathers,
her flight, the dream of home,
brown water opening twin petals
at her feet. The movie, that orange
novel, shapes of the river—mud slake
where she stands at some distance.
The campsite ebbs, now returns
like a wave. The treeline pitches
toward me, and there, a chokecherry
springs to a river tern's reach.

Before the empty plains,
spread like flat water
shoaling toward sand hills,
the first slopes, unarable,
of the dividing mountains,
the city squats above the river,
as an Indian woman at her
day's work might squat—
oblivious to the land behind her,
her hands full of the land—
red corn, dried meats, new skins.

At Rulo, Oto, Ponca, and Pawnee
camp on flats between bluff falls,
move west each morning in open trucks
to get a year's beet sugar in.

V   (as Meriwether Lewis)

Which river is this
the first or the last?

fog like the old South
rising off slow water,
enclosing swamps

Is that a waterthrush
or falling water muted?

without channel markers
we often ran aground,
and it was impossible to
know whether we were lost
until a stream ran out
or we found a landmark,
Great Falls

the deceptive waterthrush
imitating falling water

each night I read my Journals
like a novel, seeking some
inevitability of plot, a hint
of form pointing toward an end

Am I remembering or acting again,
rounding out my own last scene
with a playwright's feel for disorder?

the cabin is filled with smoke,
like a Mandan lodge in winter,
women in the corners working skins,
young men striking flint on flint,
a man of words muttering to children
in the shadows past the firelight,

the brotherhood of wars turning
their faces to the banked fire:
floors of plank, a single table
like a keelboat, but smelling
of tallow, spilt ale, Virginia tobacco,
white smoke lit by the hearth fire,
a roadhouse lost in a river fog

    tavern odors and the far-off
    drip of water, thin as birdsong;
    the swampbird singing of water
    as the great waters quickly fall;
    fog touched with a hint of
    Cyprus standing in still water
    and spruce wet with mountain rain

there is a bend in thought
as treacherous as a river's bend
forked at the farthest side;
I have forgotten its meaning,
the lesson it holds for the sailor,
devout in purpose with a mind for home,
or the thinker intent on endings uncharted,
lost in a river fog on a still night

    I am unable to make a homily stick
    and fasten my thoughts, foundering, to it,
    unable to make a sighting certain enough

the river has neither course nor current;
the last point of the relative compass,
upstream/downstream, falls away; the duet
of waterfowl and waterfall, complimentary
virtuosi of distances untaken or taken
and forgotten, is joined to dissonance.

VI

Tonight, the Mare Tranquillitatis,
like a thumbprint on silver,
and oddly, like a street name
or an address, the Plain of Jars.

"This feather stirs . . ."

wind's wing across water,
something brushed aside,
the care taken, her eyes;
what we had imagined in
the trees, as though witnessed
at it and afterwards feared
so many things otherwise
common, the quickness
of small animals, birds,
dragonfly and cicada.

Quiet takes back her
folded fields. Elmshoot,
chokecherry and willow
clamor above shadowed
watermillions, the Leek-
green grass, buffaloberry,
"which strikes & profumes
the sensation," those busy
tides, treacherous sand—
how it swirls and gathers
where rivers join—
the Platte's due payment,
distant soil "with great
velocity roleing," as though
the high plains in visitation . . .
the bitter places, destinations
we already have names for,

all that is said of what
most surely awaits us,
wind and water, this green
tumult, its weathers.

Think of the clouds
as surfaces in time,
the river bank as
a banking of clouds,
that what is seen here
folding over itself
is a gathering of those
pasts we voyage into
and so watch it all
with practiced apprehension.
This peculiar edge of things
wears toward us at its
own pace, the scree
of distant mountains
configured now as leaves.

Marsh of Sleep, Sea of Crises,
Sea of Serenity, Lake of Dreams.

VII

Among the provisions they carried
across tidal drifts of sand
and wind drifts snared with weeds—

hemp-bound faggots dipped in pitch
and flax-bound sheaves of grain;
so the land was parceled first

in cross-stands raised on a salt
beach, each household counting its
remaining necessities, thus counting

the lands they were wedged into—
sweet soils beyond salt bogs
and stiff grasses. Rivers, trails

where Spanish armor rusted into
dark mud. What they had expected
was a magic, wholly accessible, devout

as daylight, gold the western sun
displayed, cities of gold, resplendent
in that holy fire. In a tangle of

purpose—dream and vision—there
were many caught in this soil, clutched
down among their metals, decaying.

VIII   ("signs is *signs*, mine I tell you")

Time and time again, snake's
head rising to the doe's
udder, and her, fresh-killed,

hanging over the water
and no great distance from it.
I threw chunks and drove

this snake off Several times;
was so determined, I was
compelld to kill him. Peeled

Some bark to lay down on,
gathered wood to make fires,
Heard the party on shore.

So much always moving away.
Be quick about it! Fond
farewell, watery grasp. You

rest your head one evening
against the powdering sand,
say a few words, murmur

to the gathering dark—
umbruliata, the enshadowment,
trees' long slant, hillside

and what lies beyond, that
brightness faltering, as well.
Broad expanse of the river

turned to blood, red hue
drifting into gold or boiled
with rings, many-tinted as

an opal. Graceful, smooth
circles uncoil each syllable;
what was said to her, embossed

in gold, crept by me upon
the waters: colors of departure—
sunset, the stars' terrible retreat.

Centered, now, by all that leaves
us behind, its red calibrations,
our lines of sight played like

taut strings, the present moment
trembles within other durations—
that clay, as though precisely

cut, its remnants swirling fire
at my feet, the galled leaf
flared from a bare stem,

snake's head or flame dancing.
Light-play and murmur acquiesce
to image and parable, that tongue

flicking, our own incessant song,
how carefully the ship's pilot
steers past its raptures, dangers

the beauty shimmers here—
bluff reef, break, changing
channel and dissolving bar—

all that the castaway holds
dear, drifted . . . drifted
precipitate of his bewilderment.

IX

The sunlight on the water,
landfall shadows, treeline
edging down the slow current.

This is the land I made for you
by hand, what was touched once
then misremembered into words,

place where the soil slips out
from under its trees, where
stiff weeds fall like rapids.

It is the made emblem of time,
that only, nothing we have,
nothing we have ever held,

and it is only my arrogance
that calls it mine, this press
of clay on clay, this sluice

for cattlepens and sewers.
So, sunlight yellows on water;
treeforms blacken at dusk.

"Meanwhile the voice continues,"
or several voices, mine, yours,
those others that slide beneath us

among catfish and bullheads
angling in the slime, water voices
that suck the current in and pump it out,

gills that speak back waters the river's
long swirl threads to oblivion,
and her voice somewhere in the rocky

watershed, as yet unformed, thrilling,
who speaks in tongues so quickly, child
at the sunny edge of constant snow.

X   (In and Out)

In came the doctor,
in came the nurse,
in came The Lady
with the alligator purse.

That moving window of rope,
the hazed shape that swings
boundaries or hazards.
                              Once
he lived here, often taking
a morning walk or afternoon
stroll along this street.

Did you know her once,
forgotten, The Lady?

Surgical implements and appliances
still-lived on the porcelain table,
the delicate tubes that feed and drain,
hang translucent curves, coaxial;
a flexible bedside straw angles from
a smudged waterglass like a cut stem.

She held her gloves in one hand,
the limp fingers spread like petals,
dark and wilted, above her fist;
beneath her dress, where her crossed
legs pressed tightest, she ground
nylon on nylon into another breath.

They count in song
or sing the alphabet,
adding syllables to match
the jostle of their step.
In verses some words
are merely breath;

silences
are sometimes spoken.

Go in and out the window.

The rope's click on the pavement
springs the half-circle out of shape;
the projector loop stutters and
Pasolini dances:
Il mondo salvato dai ragazzini,
toe caught and falling through
the flickering hemp casement.

"the descent beckons . . ."

She cranks the head up
and turns his face to the window—
late light sluiced past
chokecherry across occluded eyes;

the brown water threads its sludge;
the sprung branches of a fallen elm
trail curls of yellow scum, turning
as the catheter bends southward.

"there warn't no home
like a raft, after all"

Each spring the land spills back
with the receding floods, the slag
of the gray flats hooked with rubble,
stiff weeds strung with drying mud;
the river's harvest bobs in the dark current.

Her hair swings and jostles
the dance the mud encloses—
coagulated drops slowing the turns,
thick chokecherries bead the light.

"At Malvern, the trees . . ."
Thwaites, Jim, Buckeridge,
Gutheridge, the fisherman,
Lewis, the birdman;

the woman, expecting flight,
as she calls the river's slow turns;
the Lady, shifting in her chair,
pulling the strings of her beaded sack,
snapping the florentined, flowered clasp,

click, the recessional: song and dance.

Out went the doctor,
out went the nurse,
out went The Lady
with the alligator purse.

II

Tracings

"The women were divided between
regrets for the homes they had left
and fear of the deserts and savages
before them."

Francis Parkman

nothing but this continent
intent on its dismay—
hands, etc. bandaged,
a torn petticoat fringed
with lace, roseate frozen
fingers, or elsewhere
feet wrapped in burlap
scuffing new snow

after the indigo of their tunics
seeps back into the soil
this spring, the several springs'
dulling thaw and incidental greenery

what marks they made were
harrowed out by those who settled,
so set themselves against the land

whether to keep the land
open to passage
or parcel it to the plow
Benton and Everett argued

"English tartars," some said,
white savages to plunder the trade,
"only farmer and tradesman stabilize"

his head raised slightly
the dying woodsman
views the open plains,

"flat water" squalls
spilling stiff grasses
into the small shade a stand
of scrub trees gives his end

"huge skulls and whitening
bones of buffalo
were scattered everywhere"

the Conestoga's canvas
straining to the wind,
the plow's first bite,
the first indenture
of the rutted road,
crossties set down,
oil, asphalt glittering
quartz aggregate to the sun

the harrow's bright discs
crumble the damp shine
of the new furrow,
the wind dulls and sifts
grassland into dust

two days in the storm cellar,
wet rags to their faces,
the slatted door impacted
with wet rags, dowery linens

strange light at the cyclone's
onset, a cupped brightness
edging banks of dark clouds,
fields darkening in lines
of gathering dust, section
on section spilling eastward,

a straw drilled through a tree,
a team of mules transported
forty miles intact

a dream of transport, Dorothy
soaring on the wind, becalmed
in still another summer, lost,
follows billboards and Burma Shave
into the city's ragged sprawl

Uptown or Lakeview, five
children in three rooms, A.D.C.,
weathers like unpainted wood,
stacked porches where her laundry
tatters with city grit, bars
haunted by banjo music

everybody talks of home
as though it were the sparkle
of an earlier dream, a glint
of rainwater in someone's hair,
names you can't remember,
old photographs gone brown
with age, a man and woman,
faces obscured by broad hats,
a bare tree beside them,
the bare distances empty
and faded into the sky

Oxus, Phasis, Palmyra—
Oz encased in glass,
"variegated with fields and meadows"
store window dioramas
display the life and manners
of high-rise glass apartments—

The El Dorado, Malibu East—
warm winters, cool summers
high above the city's noise

clouds move in facets
across their polished faces,
tipped red at sunset, presiding
over a close-set clutter
of flat, graveled roofs

graceful as mannequins
they are laughing into
the summer evening, women
bright as spring flowers,
in autumn's colors,
warmed and smiling,
they talk of love
before a dying fire

gray as she is, aging,
she fingers the pictures
of ladies' magazines,
fingers, as well, pictures
she brought from home

the red flowers on the floor
wear into black treads, black
dust comes in at her windows

his weapons arranged at his side,
the sun darkening his sight,
Cooper contrived his death
in alien spaces; Boone finished
his days on a crumbling porch
that fronted on the open West

Reeving

Tricks of the weather
or slights of memory,
another Sunday empty
of touch, so clear
this January seems like May.

Impositions of dead fathers,
their remaining tyrannies—
the Dutch-German I never knew
panning for gold or harrowing
South Dakota into dust, quick
flashes of amethyst across
the blackened winepress
when late sunlight reaches
my grandfather's cellar,
hard spring of plowseat,
the dying gambler in black
coughing into his cards
or oiling the blue sheen
of his stub revolver.

More, certainly, than is needed,
these insistent returns—
as though the flat of Nebraska
were closing like a hand,
the rivers we have lingered by
spilling out through life-line
and love-line, the lines
of fortune and trade,
the slough of old soil.

Only the dust of hands,
season on season, what
gathers in the boot of
an empty silo or sifts

into the widening lines
of a rough-cut floor,
gathered back to haze
the city in, salt streaks
across dry pavements,
winnowings of a long winter.

After-Milking

(burden of that hyphenation,
what fulcrum for the quartered
moon on some dairy's calendar)

lay silent there, waiting speech,
the hay dust sifting down
through the rough-cut floor

call it cowstain, the must
that grows upon old wood
like lichen, blossoming with age

indefinite children, lost farms,
still the straw points caught
in your trousers itch and sting

and the gag of warm milk catches
just where the words begin, you
swallow it back and start all over

Materials of June

Clear vials of cloudy
sputum on a windowsill,
the hand they said I saw
waving from a balcony,
that bony face of his
buoyed up in tufted satin.

Three times as many years,
they sprout among the peonies,
open in the froth of new flowers,
so many petals where the features
find themselves again, floating
as the insects do their work.

Hand like a bare stem waving
in a windowbox, fingers in
the thin spread of unleaved
branches, vague arms in shadow.
Overnight the dandelions
have coughed up their seeds.

They are spinning in the air
like phlegm in draining water
until the grass snags them still
or you suck them in with your breath;
they root down there, forked tubers
with hair-thin tubercles extended.

Blind Pew

"nowhere to go, nothing to see"
we are all tired of the news,
wait each night for the end,
the newsman's cardiac arrest

"you might as well come quietly"
these days our consolation is
that we might be the last to go;
this is also a matter of rivers,

the man at the button going first,
dissolving into his pointed finger,
so much spring snow feeding a small
stream, stream to river, river to sea

too many clues, too much to remember,
an odd recitation we make or hear
set down as evidence, nothing in the way
of declaration, not a public statement,

but that someone, certainly childish,
ourselves in another guise, may act
on it, might set out for distant
places, dreaming of gold and silver

Five Songs in Sequence

i

begins there
among hands,
as though by
accident
and wanders
by its own
turns, discovers
or lies still

ii

you thought it
had been designed,
proceeded by some
strategy, going
from left to right
and as usual
downward
in and among

iii

so many years,
the car creaks cold,
the movie I
want to neglect
tangles its own
bodies, heaps them
against surf,
landing-craft flap
open, they charge
through seawater
fountained with shells

iv

take it from there,
late spindrift of
old leaves, rollers
heave his shoulders,
his back arches
above flotsam

v

how is it we
always know who's
going to die,
how he will run
across the beach,
how the tracers
will rush to meet him
or speed along his
footprints splashing
sand, the one who bit
his lip, the other
who talked of home;
we stir in our clothing,
almost ready to be
afraid, slouch back
and breathe small passions
into an already
interrupted night

The Judy Travaillo Variations

for Eugene Wildman

"Of course the other one looks just like her,
but if you really know her, you can tell
the difference even at a distance."

I

There is always the other one
pushing a cart in the supermarket
or standing on a corner waiting
for you to make the obvious mistake,
begin, that is, a smile and catch
yourself halfway, leaving your face
just that much in disorder, no chance
to recover yourself or turn away.

The problem and the test, knowing her
enough—the eyes, perhaps, certainly
not just the hair which shifts and tangles
or the posture that is put on and primpt;
that dress she wore once, the other might
take by stealth or even bargain for,
the one making the other herself briefly
in exchange for certain favors, anonymity,
of course, and possibly her own confusion
somehow relieved, the other wearing it.

And no one, knowing the facts of the case,
would blame you, knowing the disorder
she settles in upon you, the choice
you sometimes make, wanting only choice,
and after all the retreat is expected—
who wouldn't, knowing what you know—
and is judged only when she, the other,
takes your absence as her success.

II

For three weeks
among high lucerne,
saw them grazing like
cattle in familiar meadows,
birds bobbing their heads,
prized mostly for their feathers.

Lunch at the Royal Albertinia,
the consommé springing to the spoon,
the tea thick with mint leaves.
On the veranda talk of a trek
north along the coast.
The natives, they say, have
their women in common,
covering their bodies
with warm red clay,
all their wives becoming,
as the clay dries to powder,
the one wife they can share.

Whitney says this mission
requires more soap than sermons.

III

The arms and legs of Chicago—
fingers that push hair back
from the face, pick clothes
away from wet skin, the face
relaxing as the first air in hours
is drawn in between and expelled,
grit darkening the creases of the neck,
grinding like pumice behind the knees.

Her back to you, swaying with the train,
fine hair clotted with sweat, hand
passing, occasionally, under it.

IV

A cut-out Eskimo in cardboard
spells it out in frost, COOL INSIDE,
icicles hanging from every letter.
In the darkness the chill settles
down on your neck like a wet cloth.

If he had an airplane or a car,
could trail white vapor into ice
clouds above the tangled streets
or glide like a landlord through
the city toward country-club cocktails
and summer evenings with Lizabeth Scott;
if he had not begun so badly, desiring
so much, not taking it all with boredom,
tossing his cufflinks onto the dresser
from a bedroom chair, dinner jacket
sprawled across the carpeted floor.

It is hot tonight, she says, turning,
offering her zipper to his hands.

V

Lost again, strayed from the picnic grounds,
they should have tied him to a tree.
Alone, his Indian companion or the dark-
eyed lady from the grocery store
gone back for supplies or help,
breechcloth or lace panties drift
down the sluggish stream; he fishes
it out with a branch, remembering
his devotion and her eyes when they parted.

III

News Notes, 1970

for John Matthias

i

and the bottles   rocks flew
Grant Park   the yachts still
lolling their slow dance of
masts and flying bridges
tear gas   a few gunshots
evening papers tally the costs
in police cars   fashionable windows
several injured   none dead
fear a new alliance beginning
"the brothers and the longhairs"
"mellow," one said   surprised

ii

music from a flat guitar
its neck angled across
his crotch like a gunbelt
right arm almost straight
music like the stone extended
reports through the microcircuit
concussion registers rock
against a head just turned
the tallied windows   cars
overturned and burning
a mellow swirl of bodies
breaks over the ear like music
fades out with evening
echoes only in newscasts
prolongs a traffic jam

iii

if we could name each part
pick through every archipelago
the city's wash contains
species that waddle
history through the streets
islands brush past us
their clatter gathers
volume   then subsides
the landscape dips and curves
notes for a full catalog
curl in the fire
new explosions contend
with old salvage   sludge
the air we crouch in
expecting martial music
beating through the drone

iv

for two weeks studying
a handspan of spruce
extrapolating glaciers
the silt this limestone
still imitates   breaking
into flat shelves   lines
the receding waters left
trees rooted in their faults
pine pitch fills the air
a cardinal flares in the brush
moving against its greenery
as water moves against stone
closing off this valley's
tumbling progress with
repeating crest   break-over

ebb   and sounding fall
as ice moved a millennium
as the earth moved   extruding
silt compacted into stone
as we move now   compacted
shouldering buildings into
place   hefting post and lintel
shouldering it all down
cities   valleys   plains
the intricate dance of greenery
we presumed the world at rest
tread into a widening slag

Prothalamion

Presume for the day
    that the weather has turned
        for you, bending in your arms
as you might bend
    finding each other comfortable,
        each seeking the other's shape,

that fingering the flowers
    of your own household
        you warmed the corollas
of field flowers in *Prairie du Chien*
    opening dandelions to a gray sky
        bluebells to bare soil.

Say each wind is a breath,
    the late gathering of clouds
        the close commerce of your sleep.
The broomgrass has a liquid ease
    spilling green waves to the sun as
        birch leaves flash their silver undersides.

The old lady of summers
    grazes in flat spaces where
        trees spread out like petals
gathering her song and dance
    from our shufflings toward gaiety
        her purpose in our presumptions upon her.

Pine Trees with Child

for Francesca

Waft, wave,
the pine fronds,
limestone where
lakewater curls over
and, sounding, falls
under spread branches,
green haze, blue eyes,
the child I hold up
into the sunlight,
thinned and shifting,
nymph flies spinning by.

We begin to forget ourselves,
are almost casual; two jays
clatter blue wings upward,
three quick slaps, only
the widening ripple, perhaps
the dark body's single flash
as the fish falls back,
thus reasoned into place.
We can not help supposing.
Eyes wide, she turns,
head following just that
part of it, some span
of this day's moving.

Four Postulates

for Anselm Hollo

I

what is most valued,
the cherished things
any moment in Iowa
settles so carelessly
upon you—cat stickers,
a coded signal Home
Orange Juice is trucking by,
some morning or any day
when winter spring summer
and the poem begin again

II

who was it started laughing?
someone otherwise somber,
the Christmas lariateer
spinning double circles,
dancing through the lasso
at his side, bullwhipping
cigarettes from his lovely
assistant's scarlet mouth
every hour on the hour
next to the howling Santa Claus

III

would have thought other-
wise, conceded the point
at first argument; of course
there were mornings, the hills
went on to Cedar Rapids
and Davenport; in its own season
the corn's pollen stung another
hand; brown rivers paled with ice;
those were the truck washes we had
known before, the spit of gravel
from the humming wheels; the patient
customer of truck stops knows the best
of these returns, hulks them into
the dark of his coffee with rounded
shoulders and extended forearms

IV

it is the line of force or the vector
that sees us through our ambiguities,
diagram of rivers, path the semi
takes among its various winds, turn
the night makes at a neon sign, EATS,
locus of all points on the lasso's rim,
itself remembered; somehow each of us
knows the double twist of brittle fiber
that holds the line together, knows
the turns the rain takes, heaves
the long land rests against our feet

The Edge of Autumn

The wind, a rustle of leaves
and brown hair fanned out, strand
by strand into blown leaves—

a light squall across littered
grass, a shimmering of leaves
and brown, blown hair.

A radio plays beneath a static
of leaves, dark maple, yellow elm—
Everytime we meet, everything is sweet,

and meeting, leaf-strewn, soft-
edged in a shelter of blown leaves,
her hair is drawn out by a soft wind,

and the radio plays the rhythm
of his hands sweetly across her
leaf-strewn back. From the black

plastic case, through dry leaves,
the news from Bien Hoa; it says,
one grieves at the thought of men

sprawled among rubble,
while the lovers, here,
cresting on a wave of leaves,

rubble at a season's edge,
strain to a memory of music,
the lasting rhythms of an insistent dance.

Shadow Puppets

Against a room's neutrality
we cast the threat of words,

almost forgotten, how condition
and consequence gather whatever

shadows are available and gnarl,
ourselves gone strange at the edges:

a game for a child's bedtime,
the fox and the goose, their bright

geography, wingspread and mouth
gaping, a play of grace and need.

After Neruda

against blue moving
sea-blue, and against sky-blue,
some yellow flowers

October arrives

there with the sea's
great purpose,
its myth, its mission, its ferment,
the gold place
of a single yellow flower
sparkling
explodes over the sand,
and your eyes catch on the earth,
just a moment's rest
from the immense sea

we are dust, will always be

neither air, nor fire, nor water
but
earth
only earth
always
and perhaps
some yellow flowers

Lessons in Light

for Fred Maurice

Monet

it buoys them up, floats
ironwork off its pillars,
lifts stonework, arches
the footbridge into air,
loosens everything;
the waterlilies dance
in sunlight above water

Fitz-Hugh Lane

all lit from within
the beached cutter's hull,
ragged shoreline, the bay's
barrier of bright stones,
fresh as a new world
we only imagine—
quandam lucem,
a kind of light

Hopper

heavy in the light
that yellows her room
at angles, she weighs
upon herself like
a building or a bridge—
apparent stress, shoulders
hunched forward, arms
bearing their load downward
into raised knees, feet
and buttocks held firm

Albers

spin any of them
at the center and
the colors whiten
away, an early
lesson, one color
only and its varied
absences

Enderby

Today already afternoon—
not so subtle, things pass
not always one by one, more
often clumped into rush hours,
minutes, the leaves, photons,
I imagine, cresting where
a shadow is ridged across
the windowledge at my feet,
waves without surface taking
themselves to this edge, others;
to think that those lines, too,
are threaded in every direction,
waft of light out there, the haze
deepening. It is autumn.

Primary Exegesis

Nothing more than was
warranted by her song,
incautious morning,

occasional bits
we thought that day
could be gathered

up like bachelor
buttons, late spring
nosegay, nothing more.

In time you notice
the colors seeping
from the dahlias

staining the glass,
and the day darkens
there, and it will not

come clean, the whole
winter's diligence
at smaller things,

morning sunlight
caught by crystals
that grow in from

the edges of the glass
like plaited leaves,
so garlanded, chill blue

perfecting the air
to sharp sounds,
the wind and its metals.

She presses her hand
to it and the warm air
displays a moist corolla

that lingers and fades,
returns in slant light,
the first measure, some-

thing extended eventually
to fit my own hand,
its palm opening the day.

Lumen

"Yearning and dying"
those old songs in
so many voices—

so warm today,
litter of sooted snow,
salt-streaked pavements,

some talk of seedlings
for spring planting
windowbox fuchsia.

"No paroxysm, inward,"
this practical love
toward what unity?

Meister Eckhart, you
and your carolers
make very little

of the day's particles.
Those shafts of light
the soul is mirror to

churn with dust and lint,
are known by these only—
no radiance, *kein Wesen*.

The rich petals spread
downward purple and red,
flesh and vesture still.

IV

Set / Sorts

Set

"if she is where the paths stop"
James McMichael

Like accidents, surely,
such centers arrange
the land to themselves—
the folds of slanting
hills, wash of spring
rains, walkways you
only happen to take—

and yet the tread
resounds into centuries
of walking back from
apparent fields
or slips into ruts
of pilgrimage or trade.

She waits, unappointed,
at a place the land
designs for waiting,
an end of paths.

What will be called
the first map of this
occasion? perhaps
the floor she scuffs
impatient for your
return, furniture
her skirts brush past,
chrysanthemums beside
the gate, blossoms
black against sunset,
the cinder path you
grind with your heels,

remnants of a plumb line
where old walls meet,
the known place where
skin moistens skin.

Sorts

I

In spaces where
touch begins, fails,
a quickening of air,

light churned round
in breaking water,
mounting waves,

that distant shore
our undercurrents
drift us toward, how

soon the sense fails
like crystal husking
its facets into some

dazzle without
weight or shape—
salt spray, this

dampness or all
yours, its wet
still settling,

that narrow wave
curling into you,
you ride as light

above its foam,
Cyprianna, yes, you
ride the afternoon.

II

In a close room,
smell of peat
from seedlings you

tend so carefully,
soft soil that
sucks its water in

with a deep breath
like air pulled
through teeth or

moist sighing,
the pale stems,
twin nymph-leaves

shaking as you
pass, gathering
your breath, mine,

together into what
freshness and our
familiar surprise.

III

Firepoints pressed into
our eyelids, the shapes
we give to darkness,

compounded of fire,
jostle like molecules,
already with us,

touch worn smooth
as a sacred stone—
so much devotion—

or sea-surge across
pebbles or river-run
gathering sweet soil;

so sleep begins,
slow wear under fire—
distant bird, beechen,

a shore, riding inward,
bluff-cut and canyon,
now a sudden geography.

IV

White water and stone,
time to speak, morning
chill against glass;

awake, some green
at a fixed distance,
a few steps from where

the dream churned itself
into air, restless foam;
said, good morning—

good morrow, some
space of the night
still damp between us.

V

Instants to our fingers,
years to the hand spread,
arms stretched toward that

vacancy, place the dream
once fully sustained,
reluctant pastoral.

VI

As though the music
fell about us, hazed
vistas, tender cinema;

grown old and weary,
past dying fall to Webern;
all said, something stops

in that landscape grown
full behind us, such
unseasonable snow—

the borders our turning
sets there, those lands
by our absence divided.

V

A Hanging Screen

"In warm sunlight jade
engenders smoke"; poetry,
like indigo mountain,
keeps its distance;

the light plays words
and figures, stone's
edge edged with air,
green haze growing.

Amused by butterflies,
Chuang Tsu dreaming,
the emperor's heart in
spring, thoroughly transformed.

Still, in pieces, the words
rest so much apart.
Risking my life I lean
on dangerous railings.

When the dream wakes
to its own particulars,
the strands scattered,
loose hair on muslin,

broken characters
the reeds make, unmake—
vague   no reason
bright   again   dark—

the sidewalk's fracturing,
damp willow twig
forked there as well
locust seedpods:

Autumn, then, and
gourd music, the wind—
indistinct   no-stop
break   again   join.

Drifting between narrow
bluffs, sharp bends
enclose us, deep
rain-cuts all around—

mountain pass, slant
sunlight and snow line,
the dream piazza
gilded into a high valley;

"haze, mist," Kuo Hsi
interrupted, sluice-
way wedged into
a mountain like a keel;

what was said by fire-
light, the bandit in
the yellow sombrero
laughing at the window.

Chill surprise of
Chinese apples, glitter
of the Pacific between
buildings—caught in

passing, an empty
rowboat or Russian sealer
riding at anchor, Magellan
full sail in dusty curtains,

casements groan like
taut rigging, bright
shore, the heat lines
full of spice, breadfruit

stretching to our hands;
a new nourishment, this
mission, or shaded rest—
Pitcairn, a century or more.

I wanted to make this poem
of silk, stretched tight
and polished, an ink wash
drifting ambiguous mountains,

words gathered like momentary
details, instances of wind
and water among loose foliage,
painting *au plein air;* that is

alive and painting a surface
of perpetual change, the eye's
return always at odds with
memory, however certain;

the wind's warp in the cloth,
pressing the brushstroke back
full of squalls, relaxing
the line out of reach.

Afternoons

Quick passage into
memory and behind
only blank spaces,

blue stain on pink
litmus or merely
known so closely

something falls away
receding from touch,
caught in the air

your fingers move,
agile water-fly
padding the surface

of what is seen
even among these
defractions, bent

pencil or warps
of a flat eye,
the wide world circling.

Ourselves

This gathering of chance,
each of us, a swirl of
occasions, flesh their
first coincidence, what

passes through us,
waiting some arrangement
of our smallest parts,
a clear space opened

into an eyepiece or a lens
and beyond, symmetry of planets,
not, finally, a geometry
spherical or plane, sweet

press of movement, place
where the space is
always closed, always opens,
eye to eye, each eye unseen;

what we brim up to each
other called vision, touch
moves so readily among
something is passing through.

Return

I

The distance back is greater
each time we settle on the journey;

it is a game of chance, this play
of time against the lay of the land,

the hills stretched flat, wheatfields
spread thin, abrupt highway towns,

brief irregularities of line, sloped
now like telephone wires at the window.

II

How will it begin,
second by second,
the strum of a taut cord,
an accumulation swirling in,
late snowstorm drifting long
shapes, snow fences bellying
like sails to its weight,
or built up, day by day,
like the glow of a glaze painting,
the light coming back through
layered strokes as luster
and curve from the still-life's
expected oranges and bottles,
or raged up like silt and rubble
with spring floods.

III

We know so little of weight,
she said, since we've come
to believe in flight,
so casually, as though lift
could measure anything at all.
Go to the corner, watch your
shadow lengthen as you pass
the streetlight, edging into
the next darkness. You push
your own contingencies before
you, carry those distances, also.

Interstate 80

The detail, of course
it quavers in our view,
like the verge we press

the highway toward,
edge of an expected
season, implied greenery,

water shimmering always
at the same distance,
ever retreating spring.

O my America! moist
hand at the wheel,
the present moment

flattened like an insect
on the windshield, traces
of color, bits of wing,

reminders of an ulterior
delicacy, the wind itself,
a quiet air transgressed.

Esthétique du Râle

What we are confused by
is hardly less relevant
than what we know,
the examined assumptions

of our meanderings into
words ordered by rank and file,
tallied, etcetera, graduated,
the quick-step and the plod,

neither incidental, neither
wholly acceptable to those
anarchies of speech that bind
us to the days we mouth,

breath to unnumbered breath.
And yet the perfection of speech,
tyrannical dream, a fine sibilant
opening that white space just there,

as a single leaf defines a field of light
and light curls at the leaf's edge,
each, in turn, the other's hypothesis,
amused fingers amid amorous conversation,

how the tree veins itself to the touch.
It all goes on like an afternoon,
something past into which we propose
these other occasions, habitual landscape.

It is highly unlikely that the question
of touch itself will be resolved in our
lifetimes, the problem of the eye's
skittish focus, a simple unreliability

in objects each of us knows by heart,
each proliferating daily. What song?
"a single image," a lifetime played
among light and surface, on edge

and falls silent. Old *crystal acorn*,
what is there left to break away,
only the husk of clarity
and brightness alone unfurled.

Something is ending, as though
the weight of combinations,
the spread pigment we give
the universal gray—think of

the houses faceted yellow and red
into the simplest hills, another's
sense of fabric, bright arabesque,
the extended dialectic surfacing

a single guitar, insubstantial
as graphite to the touch, a casual
movement among flat particles, sheaf
of paper slipping just now from your hand.

They have taken to heaping dirt
in abandoned places, firing kitchen
matches, Buck Rogers fashion, at
their wives. Perhaps it was too much

to ask them to resolve our difficulties;
they seem unduly nervous and afraid.
Even the paint—how elegant it is!—
seems to want to fall away with each

passing semi-trailer truck. We know
how the day went, the guest list
of the party down the road, the Cadillac's
fish-tail and impact, have seen the lunge

slow-motion, chest pushed forward,
arms out, the head's brief hesitation,
bits of color settling with city dirt.
Somehow it matters more than its irony,

the fragile surface, commemorating chance.
It is only in isolate flecks, swift
and mutable, light finds its shape,
all that the form fails to exclude,

the almost unbearable clamor, every
gesture ambled among traffic, this day
or any other, talk settling in with the
portioned words, meant, I think, to be

a flower, a field of flowers, where
the wreckage seems oddly comfortable,
a seaside morning dew over bent metal
and blue Quaker ladies, *le dernier cri.*

On "The Riversongs of Arion"

The Arion of this sequence is a contemporary who sets off on a trip down the Missouri River from Omaha and gets stuck just south of the city. On July 22, 1804, Lewis and Clark proceeded north from the mouth of the Platte River about ten miles and pitched a five-day camp, named, for Silas Goodrich's catch of July 24, White Catfish Camp. This Arion's diversions, complaints, and plaintiff anthems while stranded opposite what he supposes is that campsite comprise the sequence.

I have relied heavily on Reuben Thwaites's *Original Journals of the Lewis and Clark Expedition* and on portions of his *Jesuit Relations* and *Early Western Travels*. The sequence also owes a debt to Paul Russell Cutright's *Lewis and Clark: Pioneering Naturalists* (University of Illinois Press). My personal debt to Henry Nash Smith is deepened here, as well.

Captain Clark was the most prolific diarist in the early stages of the journey, and I have often retained his peculiar spelling as a key-signature of his idiom. The notes that follow deal primarily with matters that grew familiar in the course of this sequence's journey but which are not commonly available.

I. "silver tankers": Offut Air Force Base is situated on the hills over the river near the site of the Lewis and Clark camp.

III. "the always restless . . .": from Conrad Aiken's poem "The Kid."

"Terminus": Both Thomas Hart Benton and Melville (*Clarel*) invoke the Roman god when discussing the end of American expansion at the Rockies.

"Lincoln County . . .": Billy the Kid distinguished himself in the Lincoln County Wars, though the gunslinger here is an amalgam which includes Billy, John Wesley Hardin, Wild Bill Hickok, and a smattering of movie cowboys.

"two sixes to beat": the last words of John Wesley Hardin.

"a border roll": Hardin's favorite trick, in which sixguns extended in surrender were instantly flipped back into firing position.

IV. The confusion over Sacajawea's first association with the Lewis and Clark expedition has its source in movies and popular novels, which have often presented her as an Indian "maid" who joined the explorers near St. Louis.

V. Whether Lewis was murdered or committed suicide at Grinder's Stand, Tennessee, in October, 1809, is still a matter of speculation. At his death Lewis was governor of Louisiana Territory, enroute to Washington and then Philadelphia, where he was to have edited the *Journals*.

VIII. "signs is . . .": Jim to Huck, *Huckleberry Finn* (Chapter "The Last").

The story of the snake and the doe is Captain Clark's (June 23 & 24, 1804).

umbruliata: Calabrian Italian for dusk, enshadowment.

"Broad expanse . . .": cf. Twain, *Life on the Mississippi* (Chapter 9).

X. *Il mondo salvato dai ragazzini* ("The world saved by the children"): Pier Paolo Pasolini.

Much of the identification between the river, death, and the past comes from Confucius. An example is quoted by Mao Tse-tung in his poem "Swimming":

> Here on the river the Master said:
> Dying—going into the past—is like a river flowing.

(Willis Barnstone, tr.)

Poetry from Illinois

History Is Your Own Heartbeat
Michael S. Harper (1971)

The Foreclosure
Richard Emil Braun (1972)

The Scrawny Sonnets and Other Narratives
Robert Bagg (1973)

The Creation Frame
Phyllis Thompson (1973)

To All Appearances: Poems New and Selected
Josephine Miles (1974)

Nightmare Begins Responsibility
Michael S. Harper (1975)

The Black Hawk Songs
Michael Borich (1975)

The Wichita Poems
Michael Van Walleghen (1975)

Cumberland Station
Dave Smith (1977)

Tracking
Virginia R. Terris (1977)

Poems of the Two Worlds
Frederick Morgan (1977)

Images of Kin: New and Selected Poems
Michael S. Harper (1977)

On Earth as It Is
Dan Masterson (1978)

Riversongs
Michael Anania (1978)

DEMCO